calm

the little book of colour healing

the little book of
colour healing: calm

CATHERINE CUMMING AND DEBORAH ITALIANO

MITCHELL BEAZLEY

First published in Great Britain in 2002 by Mitchell Beazley,
an imprint of Octopus Publishing Group Limited,
2–4 Heron Quays, London E14 4JP

Commissioning Editor: Emma Clegg

Executive Art Editor: Auberon Hedgecoe

Senior Editor: Lara Maiklem

Editor: Barbara Mellor

Designer: Jo Long

Picture Researcher: Sarah Hopper

Indexer: Kathleen M. Gill

Production Controllers: Alex Wiltshire and Kieran Connolly

ISBN 1 84000 585 8

A CIP catalogue record for this book is available from the British Library

Typeset in Frutiger
Produced by Toppan Printing Co. (HK) Ltd.
Printed and bound in China

contents

introduction

Colour is a quality of light, and the source of all natural light is the sun – an awesome inferno constantly pouring energy into our atmosphere. We all need light and the lack of it can have a profound effect on us.

If natural sunlight is not present in sufficiently high quantities, the result can be a potentially serious depressive illness known as Seasonal Affective Disorder (SAD), a condition that affects, to some degree at least, millions of people living in environments deprived of sunlight. The simplest way to experience the health-giving aspects of coloured light is to expose yourself to the sun. Natural daylight contains all the rainbow's hues, which is why it is such an important part of a healthy and healing home.

Each specific colour has particular qualities, and can be used for a variety of treatments that very much depend on the individual. In general, blue is the colour for calm. Like a clear summer's sky, it is infinite and heavenly. Blue is expansive, and

like the sky draws us out to space and opens us up to peace and relaxation. Blue is cooling, pacifying, and comforting and it helps us to wind down, adopt a more leisurely pace, and simply relax. Cool and deep like the boundless sea, it can transport us to the highest levels of relaxation, encouraging introspection and awareness of the depths of our subconscious. This is especially so with a very dark blue such as the midnight sky which tends to lead us into a deep dream state. Like endless space, blue is vast and unfathomable.

Blue slows the heartbeat and reduces blood pressure. We begin to breathe more deeply as it relaxes both the muscles and the mind. As a result it can be very helpful for asthmatic conditions. It is particularly healing at times when we feel anxious, restless, and worried, leading us to a serene and quiet place within. Blue helps to combat tension and ease pain. This calming energy of blue can be absorbed in many ways. Colour therapists look deeply and with sensitivity into the healing vibrations of all the different colour energies, as well as into the individual requirements of their clients – and the results of therapy sometimes have life-changing consequences. Colour healing actually works on the molecular cell structure of the

body, and as a result there is evidence of astounding success in treating different physical and psychological ailments. A typical treatment consists of exposing an individual to lights of different colours and intensities, as well as laying coloured silk over the body for a specific and monitored period of time. The reason why colour affects us on a deep level is because cells use light to communicate their bio-information to each other. In treatment with colour, which indeed is light, cells pass the healing information of a specific colour from one to another.

Since exposure to coloured light has a more powerful therapeutic effect than exposure to coloured pigment can bring about, coloured light needs to be employed with great care, even when the light is being used in the home for purely decorative purposes. Blue light is particularly calming and soothing. The effects of coloured pigment, however, should not

left: Soothing, calming blues are often used in bathrooms. Blue helps us to wind down and relax at the end of the day.

right: A large expanse of blue pigment relaxes both the body and the mind. Crisp white highlights add clarity and reflect the available light.

be underestimated as decoration often offers the opportunity to introduce large surfaces that reflect the colour with increased intensity.

There are many ways to introduce more colour energy into your home. Stained-glass panels, for example, can be used to replace plain-glass panes, or may simply be suspended in front of a window to catch the light and suffuse the room with shafts of coloured light, at once subtle and intense. Coloured glass objects can be positioned so that they both concentrate and radiate the available natural light. Glass crystals can also be hung where air currents will cause them to twirl and throw off flashes of coloured brilliance. Or you could use coloured glass bricks as translucent panels or dramatic room dividers. Simpler still, why not cover low-voltage light bulbs with coloured paint and enjoy the soft glow that they emit.

left: Filtering light through a translucent medium, such as a coloured glass panel, is an ingenious way of introducing colour into a room.

right: Blue can be perfect for bedrooms. It encourages deep rest and is very good for people who find it difficult to fall asleep at night.

colour wheel

The colour wheel, which arranges colours in their natural order, is traditionally used to demonstrate the relationship between colours and to show how new ones can be created. The three primary pigment colours (those that cannot be made from other colours) are red, yellow, and blue.

If you mix any two of the primary colours together you have what is known as a secondary colour: orange (red + yellow), green (yellow + blue), or violet (blue + red). When white is added to a particular colour, the resulting colour is referred to as a tint and when black is added a shade is produced. Tone refers to the degree of brightness. When you are decorating your home, simply being aware of the shade and tonal value of the hues that you use in conjunction with each other can help you to achieve just the right effect for balance and contrast. The composite picture opposite shows the colour balance within the main colour wheel.

Colours that are positioned directly opposite each other on the colour wheel – orange and blue, for example – are known as complementary colours. These hues are also almost opposite to each other in character. When one dominant colour is used in a scheme, the eye naturally craves the relief and balance that can be achieved simply by introducing a splash of its complementary somewhere within the room. Blue is the primary colour that sits between red and green on the colour wheel. On the red side, it takes on a lavender hue. On the green side, it becomes a cooler shade of turquoise. The wheel opposite shows a range of blue hues, tinted with white towards the edge of each colour on the wheel.

light versus pigment

Coloured light and coloured pigment are very different in the way that they react when mixed together. The three primaries of light are red, green, and blue/violet, producing secondaries of yellow (red + green), turquoise (green + blue/violet), and magenta (red + blue/violet). If all three are mixed together, they produce white light. By contrast, if all three primaries of pigment are mixed they form black. Although coloured light is far more powerful than coloured pigment, pigment colours are still extremely potent.

chakras

Chakras are the power centres through which primal energy – white light from the sun – is drawn into the body via our aura to nourish and sustain our existence. Primal energy is the force necessary for all growth.

The seven major chakras are located at different points in the body, from the base of the spine to the top of the head, although their positions may vary slightly from person to person. In addition, many minor chakras exist – for example, in the fingertips, feet, shoulders, and hands. Chakras are not physical entities, but since they link the body and psyche they exert a powerful effect.

The word "chakra" comes from *chakrum*, the Sanskrit word for "wheel", which reflects the fact that chakras are constantly moving and continuously absorbing currents of energy. Each chakra is sensitive to a specific wavelength, or colour component, of what we call "white" light. The major chakras draw in the main colours of the rainbow (see opposite), which

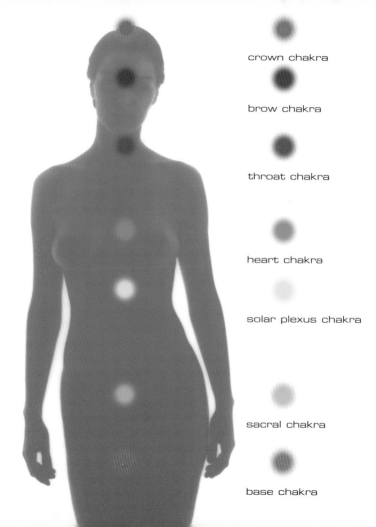

crown chakra

brow chakra

throat chakra

heart chakra

solar plexus chakra

sacral chakra

base chakra

are absorbed and then circulated throughout the body. In a healthy person, the chakras take in and distribute this energy evenly – free-flowing energy is essential for health and wellbeing. If, however, an energy imbalance exists, it is likely that either too much or too little of a specific colour energy is present. The need for different light colours is highly individual, varying from person to person.

blue: throat chakra

The physical expression of this chakra is related to creative expression in speech, writing, and the arts. The throat is the location of sound, vibration, and true communication. A healthy throat chakra indicates somebody who is able to know when and how to communicate in the best possible way. This implies integration, peace, truth and knowledge, honesty, and a kindly nature. Blockages in the area of this chakra can lead to communication and speech problems and also to feelings of withdrawal, the "blues", depression, apathy, inertia, melancholy, and introversion. As well as the throat, the governing organs of this chakra are the thyroid, parathyroid, hypothalamus, and mouth.

the rainbow

When light passes through droplets of moisture in the air, each tiny envelope of water can become a prism.

Colour therapy utilizes the fact that each major colour of the rainbow represents a different quality of light and that each vibrates at its own particular energy level.

red
relates to instinct, survival, and physical drive. It is the colour of strength, vitality, sexuality, and passion. It increases body temperature and stimulates circulation.

orange
This is the colour of joy, movement, and dance. It encourages creativity, vibrancy, and humour and is a great anti-depressant.

yellow
This is the colour of detachment and is related to objectivity, optimism, and ego. It stimulates our intellect and logical mind.

green

This colour is balancing, harmonizing, and restful. It soothes the emotions and heals the heart. It is most closely associated with nature, and of trusting in the process of life.

turquoise

This is the colour to boost immunity. It is a very cooling, youthful, expressive colour and one to relieve inflammatory conditions.

blue

This colour calms and comforts. It is restful, truthful, and peaceful. It is the colour of honesty, devotion, and aspiration. Blue slows things down, eases stress, tension, and pain.

violet

This is the colour of introspection, meditation, contemplation, dignity, and respect, and it boosts self-esteem.

magenta

The colour of letting go and moving on. It is the nurturing and protective colour of unconditional and spiritual love.

supporting hues

While the pure colours of the rainbow are the most nourishing and replenishing, other colours around us should not be discounted, as they too have their place in supporting this vibrant world of colour.

White light is an amalgam – a combination of all hues and yet none at all – and is associated with light, purity, and grace. It is clean, tranquil, and innocent. In the home, it often provides the perfect background for the range of colours used in furniture, wall coverings, floors, and decorative elements.

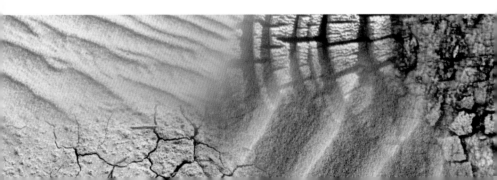

cautionary black

Reflecting none of the colour components of light, black is absorbent and so can be draining. Unlike the other hues, which let light pass through them, it does not transmit light and does not nourish us in any way.

supportive grey

When neutral grey is used by itself it feels flat and lifeless, yet it provides enormous support to the other hues.

colours of nature

The brown spectrum is grounding, supportive, and earthy. Brown is the colour of commitment and is warm and inviting.

deep blue

Deep blue is the rich, unfathomable hue of the Mediterranean sky. It carries considerable impact, containing as it does a wealth of energy. Intense and powerful, it creates a sense of calm.

Blue is a primary colour and so cannot be formed by combining other colours. On the colour wheel, blue sits between violet and green and can take on the tendencies of both these colours; however, the deep blues depicted in these rooms have neither violet nor green undertones. In terms of decorating, you will find more varieties of blue than of any other colour. Blue is firmly on the cool side of the wheel and, in common with all cool colours, appears to recede from the viewer to produce a sense of space. In the home setting, deep blue is very effective when contrasted with white to reflect as much light as possible around the room.

left: Subtle and complementary orange skin tones in the picture above the bed stand out against the deep blue of the walls.

right: Two strong blues used together like this make an extremely bold statement but at the same time have a calming impact.

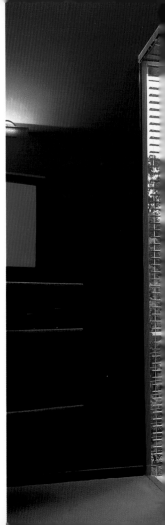

In Mediterranean countries, whitewashed buildings reflect light and heat to keep interiors cool, and buildings look whiter than white against the sky. The white of clouds against a blue sky is unfailing, purifying, and uplifting.

Good, restful sleep is almost guaranteed in bedrooms painted in a dark blue colour scheme. This colour encourages a more peaceful night and is especially helpful for those who habitually take their work home and find it difficult to switch off and relax. It also discourages nightmares and promotes better dreams. It is not, however, a colour to help get you out of bed in the morning. The version of blue shown here is particularly deep and definitely not for the sluggish, who may need a kick-start to the day – in which case it may be advisable to team up with warmer more stimulating colours.

Orange is the complementary colour to blue. and can usefully be deployed to add touches of warmth and balance. It is also a stimulating, uplifting colour associated with joy and excitement, movement and creativity.

right: Blue lights accentuate the qualities of blue, creating a deeply restful feeling. Blue is best balanced with a touch of orange.

electric blue

Electric blue is clear, clean, and gleams with a jewel-like intensity. It is extremely effective when used in small areas.

In many traditions, blues are used in kitchen and crockery decoration, and as a cooling colour for food cupboards. In a working kitchen it encourages you to take your time over preparing and eating food. In a kitchen-diner, however, it may encourage people to withdraw into themselves. Being such a cool colour, electric blue is not for rooms that receive little direct sunlight. Splashes of orange or yellow will introduce contrast and balancing warmth.

If colours become too sharp and electric, they can trigger nervous reactions. Very bright blues can become almost fluorescent in nature, thereby losing their gentle, calming qualities. Electric blue is probably the most lively of blues, and like most electric colours is often most attractive to teenagers.

left: The deep orange flowers in the blue bay of a set of units creates a striking display.

right: This shiny blue floor makes the room look larger. It also creates a floating effect, best balanced by heavier items such as books.

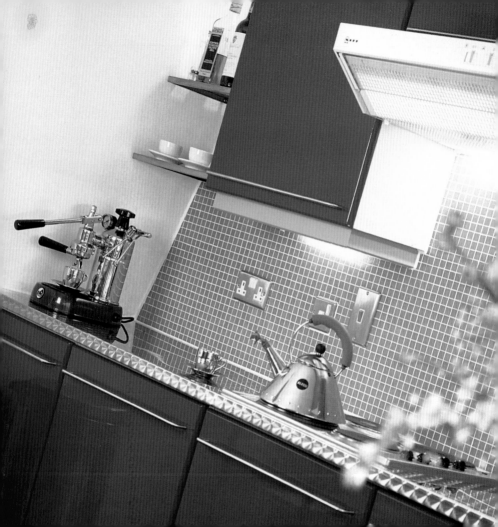

Blue is helpful for overactive conditions as it is such a calming colour. It reduces blood pressure and slows the heart beat. It also has a relaxing effect on the muscles and soothes the nerves. Its cooling influence is particularly healing for burns and sunburn. It eases tension headaches and general stress, and is particularly helpful in cases of migraine. Blue can be used to treat asthmatic conditions and it can be particularly helpful for premenstrual tension and pain – in fact blue is the best colour for easing pain of any sort.

Whether it has a satin finish or a polished sheen, this is a colour that never fails to radiate a gentle glow. Use it in association with reflective surfaces such as stainless or brushed steel to generate maximum life and energy. Electric blue is more stimulating than deeper shades, and so is a wiser choice for those of a naturally melancholic or introspective disposition.

left: In this calm, blue kitchen notice how the red light switch and the red kettle spout stand out in contrast and seize your attention.

right: Stainless-steel worktops and surfaces harmonize well with this cool blue. Reflective surfaces act like mirrors, bouncing light back and forth.

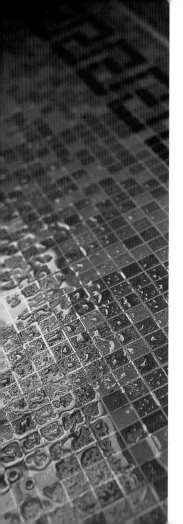

cornflower blue

The blue of this daisy-like wildflower is deep and rich, with a tendency towards the gentle, meditative qualities of violet.

We absorb colour – both colour pigment and coloured light – in many ways: through the cells in our eyes, in the food we eat, and through our skin. Cells are light sensitive, and it is known that they communicate their bio-information to each other via light. By using colour, which is light, the cells convey the healing message of each particular colour. This is why colour affects us on such a fundamental and vital level.

The bathroom, therefore, is an ideal place to take in colour directly through our naked skin every time we bathe or shower. A cornflower blue bathroom is perfect for winding down, and soaking in a tub of coloured water is a powerfully direct way of absorbing colour energy. Specialist shops sell colorant for this purpose, but a few drops of organic food dye in the bath water

left: The pure colours in this random mixture of blue mosaic tiles appear even richer and more intense when beaded with water droplets.

right: The warmth of the wooden floor and the coolness of the blue make this the perfect setting in which to unwind and relax.

will also work well. Blue's soothing qualities suit an evening bath time thus helping you to unwind at the end of a hectic day.

Soaking in a blue bathroom can recharge the throat chakra. The throat chakra is connected to expression, creativity, and imagination and so blockages here could eventually lead to difficulties in self-expression, resulting in apathy, withdrawal, and isolation. A blue bath robe worn next to the skin, meanwhile, will nourish your body with calming, creative blue energy. Choose natural fibres and experiment until you find the particular shade of blue that suits your temperament. Have fun combining colourful towels, coloured soaps, and bubble baths to create a vibrant, healing spectrum in the bathroom. Take full advantage, too, of the reflective and refractive qualities of water, which – particularly when a variety of different shades of blue are used – can suggest the sun-dappled blues of lakes and oceans.

left: One painted surface can provide just the right amount of rich blue colour energy, enhanced by clean, white woodwork.

right: With no other colours in the room, the various blue accessories in this bathroom help to create a deeply restful space.

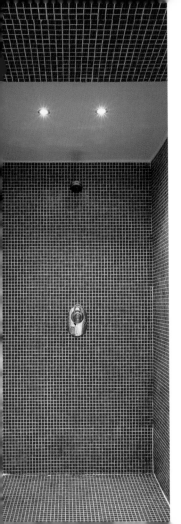

ultramarine blue

This regal blue of striking intensity is best broken up with white or used in small quantities only, as an accent colour.

Originally, ultramarine pigment was rare and expensive as it was made by grinding down the semiprecious stone lapis lazuli. Nowadays, it is a popular colour choice. The quickening pace of life means that we need to grab whatever free time there is for relaxation and de-stressing ourselves. Strong blues such as ultramarine are deeply calming and soothing, and are particularly nourishing for those who find it difficult to relax.

For the lazy and lethargic, however, excessive exposure to blue, especially the intense shades such as the strong ultramarines of the bathroom shown here, should be avoided. For them, the more uplifting and energizing colours can be a better choice, especially for a morning bath or shower. If your energy levels are already low, too much blue can result in

left: These mosaic bathroom tiles are as intense as lapis lazuli. The white grouting breaks up the colour and helps to introduce light.

right: This strong blue wall is beautifully balanced by the warm orange tones of the wooden kitchen worktop.

listlessness and inactivity, isolation, and even depression. In fact, we are all familiar with the expression "feeling blue" and, similarly, few of us are immune to the essentially sad and melancholic music known as the "Blues".

With an intense colour such as this, it is important to add balance through the use of a complementary hue, in this case orange. As blue calms and slows us down, orange lifts our spirits, stimulates, and creates a sense of movement and excitement.

By understanding our attraction to different colours and by appreciating their varying degrees of strength and levels of clarity, we may be able to gain fresh insights into our own psychological make-up and character. For example, we may find ourselves attracted to strong colours such as ultramarine at certain times in our lives, particularly during stressful periods.

left: The intensity of blue in this bathroom is such that it amplifies the illusion of recession that is a common feature of all cool colours.

right: Ultramarine is most effective when used as an accent colour. Here, two strong blues together make a bold but serene statement.

dark blue

This colour is most effective as part of a decorative scheme when it is teamed with warm colours. Applied as an accent colour, this sometimes overpowering hue can bring a sense of serenity, peace, and calm.

Just as blue has a settling effect, warm colours such as yellow and orange are uplifting. Teamed together, oranges and yellows add life and warmth to a room, and dark blue seems to fix them and hold them in place. To achieve a dramatic paint colour such as this, you might be well advised to use artists' oil, acrylic, and watercolour paints, since many of these contain a richer depth of colour, and are of a much higher quality, than you will find in ordinary household paint. In small areas these colours can be used on top of household paint to produce an especially rich and stunning effect. Try experimenting with this technique directly on

left: The dark blue of this sofa is so intense that it can be used only in limited amounts. The sofa is an ideal way to enjoy this deep dark blue.

right: As dark blue is such a strong hue, small accents, such as the glass vase on this bedside table, are enough to supply ample radiance.

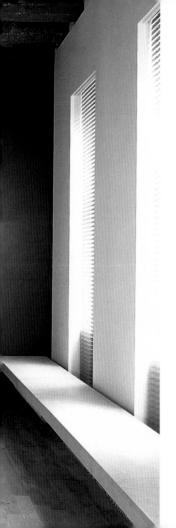

a wall, on panels, or even on canvas. Painted panels in blue are helpful in any tense environment, such as a busy or noisy office. Not merely decorative objects in their own right, they can also help to ease the stress of the modern workplace. They also have the advantage of being easy to repaint in order to create startlingly different effects in various strengths of colour and different hues to suit every circumstance and personality.

Calming blues can be used to good effect in any hectic situation, especially where people seem particularly quick to anger or there is obvious potential for impatience or conflict. In public areas, if lengthy queuing is expected – such as in a bank at lunchtime – clear, strong, bright blue can act as a salve for fraying tempers. This shade calms the nerves, slows the heartbeat and makes us breathe more deeply. It may also still erratic thought processes, and even bring a sense of trust and serenity. Choosing calm, positive colours, such as blue and its complementary warm tones, may help to create a more beneficial environment for all of us.

left: Used on only one wall this dark blue appears to push the surface further away, creating a feeling of distance.

blue splash

A striking intensity of colour can feel so supportive and nourishing. Just a splash of rich blue is often enough in a room.

Blue glass provides a magical colour when illuminated. Blue vases, glasses, or door and wall panels create short bursts of intense blue energy. Coloured glass is so effective that therapists employ it for concentrating the rays used during treatment. This needs to be carried out by a qualified practitioner, however, since adverse effects can result if the timing of a treatment and the use of balancing complementary colours are not calculated properly. There are many different methods of treating with coloured light. One such method, known as Colourpuncture, devised by Peter Mandel, involves a torchlight with changeable coloured glass filters. The coloured light is directed to acupuncture points on the body, so conveying the healing message of a particular colour. Another method of treating with

left: These cream walls provide a flexible background for changing colour schemes, focused here on the strong blue of the cushions.

right: The strong blue in these pictures appears more vibrant and powerful against the stark white walls and monochrome furniture.

coloured light, developed by Theo Gimbel, involves an instrument that emits coloured lights through specific shapes, bathing the person in a wonderful healing energy.

It is interesting to keep checking your feelings about and responses to different colours, and to look for the reasons why various quantities and strengths of colour seem to attract you at particular periods or even specific times of the day. The reasons will be very personal – we all respond differently according to our own energy levels, and the colour qualities we possess, need, and attract. Colour attractions often come and go, so replaceable accessories can serve a useful purpose. A white- or cream-coloured sofa, for example, creates a perfect backdrop for richly coloured cushions that you can easily swap around. Coloured vases, as well as pictures and rugs, also provide rich accents without being overpowering.

left: These beautiful transparent blinds act as a filter. When the sun shines, the room is flooded with a splash of calming blue light.

right: Just a coloured table cloth can make an enormous difference to the colour scheme of a room. This is a quick and easy splash of colour.

moroccan blue

Moroccan blue is a deeply intense and vibrant hue. A rich pigment creates great depth of colour. In hotter climates such as Morocco this colour is commonly used to cool the heat of the powerful African sun.

Often used on textured walls, this colour is applied in washes, layering the paint to create the required density of colour. In warmer climates such as Morocco, Italy, and Greece, this blue is almost always combined with white, creating a vibrant yet cooling energy. Used with white and other shades of blue, it lightens and cools the atmosphere. White next to blue appears lighter and brighter. Under strong sunlight, bright white can be dazzling to the eye. Moroccan blue counteracts this effect by absorbing the glare. In a blue room, as opposed to a white room, the temperature actually drops by a few degrees.

left: Cool to the touch, these ceramic floor and wall tiles combine with the painted blue walls to create a cooling walk-through corridor.

right: The walls, floors, and ceiling of this room, all painted in Moroccan blue, make it a haven from the searing heat outside.

Johannes Itten, renowned for his researches into and studies in the field of colour, undertook many experiments to demonstrate this remarkable theory, which also explores the hypothesis that while blue cools a room down, red will heat it up.

In the baking heat, Moroccan blue is the perfect bedroom colour to encourage a soothing, refreshing, calming sleep as it creates a cool haven in which to relax and unwind. However, climate and the quality of light have an enormous impact on the way we perceive and experience colour and under the gentler sun and softer light of northern climes, this dazzling blue would run the risk of appearing too harsh and even cold.

Moroccan blue is most effective when juxtaposed with translucent, jewel-like turquoise and green tones, together echoing the waters of a cool, glassy sea. As it is so unapologetically rich, it is advisable to lift it with lighter shades and touches of orange, its complementary colour. Honey-coloured wood, terracotta tiles, and ochre pots are perfect for adding balance and a touch of warmth.

left: The bright white bedlinen adds a sense of light and freshness to this room, while the wood gives a sense of solidity and grounding.

nordic blue

Muted nordic blue has its origins in the countries of Scandinavia, where the sun tends to be softer and more gentle.

Nordic blue creates a sense of space and a lived-in "mellow" look. It makes a good background colour for pictures and ornaments and can be especially effective on woodwork. To create a paint effect, new wood can be aged and distressed in tones of nordic blue: paint is applied and rubbed off in places to create the effect of natural wear and tear, and washes of umber or grey soften the effect further. Nordic blues take on the quality of a blue that has faded over the years. Bright blue furniture was once sealed with oil varnish that would yellow over time, creating a natural, antiqued green-blue tone.

Nordic blue is good for people who are very sensitive to strong colours, as this colour is not at all invasive. Although the colour is very soft, it still carries a calming and cooling effect.

left: This antiqued furniture offers an ideal way to use gentle nordic blue, the wood tones adding a touch of balance and warmth.

right: Nordic blues can also be used to great effect in contemporary schemes such as this one with painted floor and wall finishes.

It is best used in lighter, brighter rooms in order to avoid too many dull grey tones. Nordic blues can also work very effectively when used in blocks of colour, offset and so brightened up by a clean surround of white. This way the colour remains subtle and not dull. The natural earthy tones of nordic blue blend well with the colours of nature. It works well as a background and enhances the subtle colours of outdoor foliage. It is particularly suitable as an outdoor garden colour or in a conservatory.

Nordic blue is a muted synthesis of soft blue tones, the full subtlety of which can only emerge in a diffuse northern light. Often they contain within them a touch of brown or grey – perhaps the warm colours of old pinewood showing through a distressed paint finish – which lends them a mellow "antiqued" hue. Nordic blues create an atmosphere of unruffled calm and form a natural partnership with faded upholstery.

left: These shelving units add an interesting block of colour, highlighted by the surrounding clean whites of the kitchen.

right: A vibrant splash of bright red adds a welcome warmth and excitement to the still coolness of nordic blue.

airy blue

Airy blues have a light, cooling quality like the palest of warm summer skies. Light and expansive, they bring with them a feeling of spaciousness and freedom. Airy blues are particularly suitable for restricted areas.

Airy blues banish feelings of being closed in and limited, and are invaluable for making basement and underground areas feel less restricted. They are gentle, calming colours suitable for almost any room. They have the capacity to make rooms look much larger than they actually are, thus creating the illusion that the walls are receding, this makes them especially suitable for opening spaces up. A pale blue ceiling, for instance, would increase the perceived height of a room, while a narrow room could be made to appear much wider by painting the two closest walls in a pale sky blue.

left: Airy blue and white create a sense of cleanliness and space yet do not appear too cool. They are often used together in bathrooms.

right: Used in enclosed spaces with no windows or natural light, airy blue brings a sense of freedom and expansiveness.

Because these colours are so expansive and airy, they may need grounding with earthy colours, and with elements such as natural wood and stone. Like all colours, airy blues are particularly enlivened by natural sunlight, but be careful not to use them in too dark a room where they could appear a little grey and cool. As airy blues are such gentle, soft colours, they are very good for bedrooms, encouraging a calming and restful sleep. They are also suitable colours for very young children and babies, and are especially helpful and calming for hyperactive children. Many parents choose to decorate their children's bedrooms in a kaleidoscope of bright, jolly colours, but as children are very sensitive to the effects of colour, a gentle wall colour such as airy blue can work well as a backdrop. Brighter colours can then be introduced in smaller items such as pictures, toys, curtains, and furniture.

left: Painted on a sloping ceiling, this airy blue helps to push the wall back out again and avoids an enclosed, uncomfortable feeling.

right: Airy blues are most helpful for anyone who has trouble sleeping at night as they are among the most soothing of colours.

directory

These are all addresses of associations and centres that teach colour therapy.

Colour Therapy Association
PO Box 121
Chessington
Surrey KT9 2WQ
Tel: 01276 683111
www.colourtherapyassociation.com

Colour Affects
Angela Wright
908 Keyes House
Dolphin Square
London SW1V 3NB
Tel: 020 8932 6492
www.colour-affects.demon.co.uk

Hygeia College of Colour Therapy
Brook House
Avening
Tetbury
Gloucestershire GL8 8NS
Tel: 01453 832150
theo.gimbel@virgin.net

Hygeia College North Centre
4 Sunningdale Close
Kirkham
Preston PR4 2TG
Tel: 01772 261128

International Association of Colour
46 Cottenham Road
Histon
Cambridgeshire CB4 9ES
Tel: 01223 563403
www.internationalassociationofcolour.com

IRIS International School of Colour Therapy
Farfields House
Jubilee Road
Totnes
Devon TQ9 5BP
Tel: 01803 868037
www.iriscolour.co.uk

Living Colour
PO Box 27016
London N8 8ZU
Tel: 020 8347 8585
www.living-colour.co.uk

Ann Lloyd
8 Rosslyn Hill
Hampstead
London NW3 1PH
Tel: 020 7794 7064

School of Mantracolour Healing
Deborah Italiano
32 Rogers House
Page Street
London SW1P 4EX
Tel: 020 7821 1143
www.mantracolour.com

index

acknowledgments

authors' acknowledgments

The authors would like to thank all the poineers in the field of colour research, particularly Theo Gimbel of The Hygeia Studios and College, together with all the colour practitioners working to bring a new and exciting dimension to complementary medicine.

picture acknowledgments

Mitchell Beazley would like to acknowledge and thank the following for providing images used in this book.

1 Nadia Mackenzie/The Interior Archive; 2–3 Philip Bier/View/Architect: Foster and Partners; 5, 6–7 Deidi Von Schaewen; 8 Red Cover/James Mitchell/Designer: Alistair Hendy; 9 Cathy O' Clery/Narratives; 10 Red Cover/James Mitchell/Designer: Lulu Guiness; 11 Marie Pierre Morel/Marie Claire Maison; 18, 20–21, 22 Getty Images; 26 Ray Main/Mainstream; 27 Ray Main/Mainstream; 28–29 View/Dennis Gilbert; 30 Ray Main/Mainstream; 31 Marianne Majerus/Architect: Alastair Howe; 32 Ray Main/Mainstream; 33 Ray Main/Mainstream; 34 Ray Main/Mainstream; 35 The Interior Archive/Simon Upton./Theatre Director: Frank McGuiness; 36 James Morris/Axiom Photographic Agency; 37 Roland Beaufre/Agence Top; 38 James Morris/Axiom Photographic Agency; 39 Elizabeth Whiting Associates; 40 James Morris/Axiom Photographic Agency/Architect: AHMN; 41 Chris Gascoigne/View; 42 Peter Cook/View; 43 Simon Brown/The Interior Archive/Designer: Clodagh Nolan; 44–45 Chris Gascoigne/View/Architect: Seth Stein; 46 Simon Brown/The Interior Archive/Designer: Conran; 47 Petrina Tinslay/Belle/Arcaid/Architect: Iain Halliday; 48 Nicolas Tosi/Marie Claire Maison/Stylist: Julie Borgeaud; 49 Marie Pierre Morel/Marie Claire Maison/Stylist: Catherine Ardouin; 50, 51 Deidi Von Schaewen; 52–53 Nicolas Tosi/Marie Claire Maison/Stylist: Julie Borgeaud; 54 Ingalill Snitt/Marie Claire Maison/Stylist: Rozensztroch; 55 David George/Red Cover; 56 Richard Glover/View/Architect: Reading and West Architects; 57 Guy Bouchet/Marie Claire Maison/Stylist: Catherine Ardouin; 58 Jan Baldwin/Narratives; 59 Dennis Gilbert/View; 60 Abode; 61 Nicolas Tosi/Marie Claire Maison/Stylist: Julie Borgeaud.